TREADING

on

Thin Ice

Questions, every equity investor must
ask, and answers, none would get.

First Edition

Rajesh D. Mudholkar, ACMA

©Copyright 2014
Rajesh D. Mudholkar, Author
All rights reserved

Self-published
Sept 6, 2014
CreateSpace Independent Publishing Platform
(An Amazon Company)
Distributed by Amazon and its associates
ISBN: 978-1501084614

Simultaneously published
Sept 6, 2014

Intellipi Publishing
Pune, India
ISBN Pending

Contents

Prologue — i

1. Evidence of Systemic Failure — 1
2. Barricades Don't Prevent Tsunamis — 15
3. A Fatal Communication Error — 25
4. A Bird in Hand, or Two in the Bush? — 33
5. Missing the Opportunity Cost — 45
6. Fooled by the Mean — 59
7. WACC a Fallacy! — 69
8. Mind the Leverage! — 81
9. Is Budgeting Aligned to Value Creation? — 95
10. Is Value Creation Correctly Measured? — 105

Epilogue — 119

Prologue

Knowledge of how financial markets work is as important for everyone, as general knowledge about health and illness is. More so, for all those who invest their money in equity markets and rely on professional financial advisors to make their decisions.

Yet, contrary to what most financial professionals may believe and prescribe world over, the science of financial economics still does not have complete answers to the single most important question that affects financial health of shareholders, which contributes to financial crises:

How do financial markets function?

Can there be anything worse than a failure to prevent financial crisis? Do financial practices followed by companies and money-managers worldwide turn out to be the cause of the crippling illness?

That may sound implausible, because ever since the era of industrial revolution in the 18th and 19th century which also saw the establishment of the world's first business school 'ESCP Europe' in France (1819), several advances have been made in the fields of business and financial management, accounting, reporting auditing etc. The art and science of business and financial management has steadily evolved over time, enriched both in theory and in practice with several new tools and techniques for performance measurement and analysis.

Despite tremendous benefits derived from these developments, shareholders all over the world have witnessed market crashes from time to time and billions of dollars have been eroded due to financial crises and corporate bankruptcies. In some cases entire nations suffered debt defaults and faced downgrading by rating agencies, the crisis threatening their economies and causing widespread misery to their citizens.

These crises - such as the 2008 US sub-prime crises - have occurred even though sophisticated systems and regulations, as well as severe punishments for willful financial misdeeds have been setup over the years, notably the Sarbanes-Oxley Act of 2002.

Prologue

Even after five years since the 2008 crisis, and despite tremendous efforts by several luminaries spread over more than fifty-odd years towards enhancing the understanding of financial markets, many of whom honored for their work with the prestigious Nobel Memorial Prize in Economic Sciences, the 2013 Nobel Prize Committee minced no words in saying the following, even as the year's award was conferred for **'Understanding Asset Prices'**:

"....we do not yet have complete and generally accepted explanations for how financial markets function..."

That would turn out to be an understatement if one reads further into the scientific background note to the Nobel awards, which says:

'...currently no widely accepted "consensus (asset pricing) model" exists'.

Robert Shiller, one of the 2013 Laureates, has also been reported to have said:

"stock prices are particularly vulnerable to psychological biases because of the ambiguity in the true value of a stock, due to the lack of an accepted valuation model"

The committee further reports the findings of the laureates, that the **Capital Asset Pricing Model (CAPM)** (for which William Sharpe was awarded the Nobel Memorial Prize in 1990) still remains a fundamental asset-pricing model practiced as well as taught worldwide even though it has failed thousands of validation tests since early 1980s and contains an unexplained flaw.

Why do we need an Asset Pricing Model? As the words 'Asset Pricing' suggest, investors in risky assets such as equities must be able to estimate reasonably, how much an asset is worth today, given probabilistic estimates of its future stream of earnings vis-à-vis their own expectations. In other words, they must know the maximum price that should be paid for purchasing the asset today if the future stream of expected earnings were to satisfy investors' expectations.

Prologue

Asset Pricing Models are important for publicly owned companies too. Companies have to deploy shareholders' money in such projects which can produce returns to satisfy shareholder expectations. Therefore, the expectations benchmark given by an Asset Pricing Model serves as a project selection criterion as well as a benchmark for corporate financial performance.

How can project investment decisions and subsequent performance measurement be right, if the models used for the purpose are faulty? It's no surprise then, that massive amounts of shareholder wealth have been destroyed in the past because of faulty decisions. And it wouldn't be a surprise too, if a similar financial crisis erupts in the near future, unless the fundamental underlying flaws in corporate financial practices are fixed now.

It's one thing to muddle through by default and survive by chance, but quite another to prevent a disaster by design and survive by default if an unforeseen accident occurs. It's not enough that only those companies who manage shareholders' money prudently, or only those shareholders who have the financial knowledge and skills to choose such companies, create sustainable wealth. The entire financial management system must operate with reasonably foolproof standard scientific methods that protect the interests of all shareholders at large.

A disturbing truth was revealed from a survey by McKinsey titled 'Improving board governance' reported in April 2013. The survey garnered responses from 772 corporate directors, 34 percent of them chairs. It showed that directors still struggle to get their arms around risk management., boards are increasingly complacent about risks, have limited or no understanding of their companies' risks and spend just 12% of their time (which is less than what they did two years ago) on risk management.[1]

Financial risk affects everyone in the economy - companies aiming at optimum deployment of shareholders' funds, commercial banks evaluating corporate projects for lending feasibility, insurance companies who assess risks before accepting insurance proposals, common shareholders who

---

[1] http://www.mckinsey.com/insights/strategy/improving_board_governance_mckinsey_global_survey_results

make investment decisions, and governments engaged in economic policy-making.

This book aims to draw attention to the lurking risks that shareholders' funds continue to remain exposed to because of faulty methods being used in corporate financial practice. It raises fundamental questions which every equity investor (as opposed to a speculator), money managers and corporate financial officers must ask if they wish to shield equity capital from financial crises due to faulty financial theories and practices.

This is not just 'one more' academic book discussing another story about 'Financial Crisis', a subject that seems to have receded into remote corners of human memory, labeled as an inevitable random occurrence by some, and lulled both investors and finance professionals alike into believing that enough has been talked about it. There seems to be complacency that whatever lessons were to be learnt have been already learnt, preventive mechanisms have been already put in place, and the worst is over - far from it. This book is more of a clarion call that needs urgent and serious attention.

Consider the following statement in the 'Global Risks 2014 report' published by the World Economic Forum.[2]

"Fiscal crises feature as the global risk that experts believe has the potential to have the biggest impact on systems and countries over the course of the next 10 years."

Hopefully, investors, money managers, corporate finance officers, financial regulators, professional financial bodies, and government policy-makers would all take note and give a serious thought to the questions raised here and do what is necessary to fix what fundamentally went wrong many years ago, yet continues to be practiced. The answers and proposed solutions discussed here have been dealt with in greater detail in 'The Timeless Essence of Financial Science', a book based on my intensive research on this subject.

Rajesh D. Mudholkar,
September, 2014.

---

[2] http://www.weforum.org/issues/global-risks

Prologue

Treading on Thin Ice

1

Evidence of Systemic Failure

Treading on Thin Ice

Evidence of Systemic Failure

> *"I take full responsibility for the decisions that I made, and for the actions that I took. Based on the information that we had at the time, I believe that these decisions and actions were both prudent and appropriate.....As painful as this is for all of the people affected by the bankruptcy of Lehman Brothers, this is not just about Lehman Brothers. These problems are not limited to Wall Street or even Main Street. This is a crisis for the global economy".*

Anyone who heard Richard Fuld making this statement in his testimony post the collapse of Lehman Brothers would have been hard to convince that Fuld was the victim as he saw himself, rather than the villain as the world saw him.

Just after the crisis, in rare social appearances, he was heard introducing himself as: *"Hi, I'm Dick Fuld, the most hated man in America."* Richard (Dick) Fuld was a Lehman Brothers lifer and its chief executive officer for several years till Sept. 15, 2008, when the company sank into the largest bankruptcy in U.S. history, and triggered a global financial tsunami.

Richard Fuld is human, and so are the members of the US Securities and Exchange Commission and the Federal Reserve who were engaged in supervising Lehman Brothers. As Fuld stated further:

"Throughout 2008 the SEC and the Federal Reserve conducted regular and at times daily oversight of our business and balance sheet. They saw what we saw in real time as they reviewed our liquidity and funding, capital, risk management, and our mark-to-market process".

It would be a daunting task to influence skeptics to think in any direction other than 'find someone to hang'. Regardless of any degree of other factors - murkiness, manipulation, collusion by vested interests, or even policy makers conspiring for personal gains - that might be attributed to the enormous damage, it would be too far-fetched to believe that nothing could avert it. And if in fact the disaster was inevitable for uncontrollable reasons, then future recurrence should be also equally inevitable for the same reasons!

Several decades of research in economic sciences has not produced an acceptable consensus on 'understanding financial markets' or a reliable 'asset pricing model'. No robust guidelines for capital expenditure project evaluation exist anywhere in the world, even though accounting and reporting guidelines have made significant progress of which the International Financial Reporting Standards (IFRS) is a strong testimony. In this context the pain in Fuld's voice as he makes the following statement deserves careful attention in the interests of protecting our economic future and preventing erosion of shareholder wealth in the years to come.

"I feel horrible about what has happened to the company, and its effects on so many - my colleagues, my shareholders, creditors and my clients. As CEO I was a significant shareholder and my long term financial interests were completely aligned with those of all the other

shareholders. No one had more incentive to see Lehman Brothers succeed. And because I believed so deeply in the company, I never sold the vast majority of my Lehman Brothers stock and still owned 10 million shares when we filed for bankruptcy.......if I can be helpful in anyway to understand how we got here and what our country can do to move forward, I am happy to do so"

This book is not about Lehman Brothers or Bear Stearns or Merrill Lynch, the companies which were severely hurt by the 2008 financial crisis, among many others worldwide. It is about financial systems, which those in command now believe has gone wrong; or would it be an exaggeration to suspect whether the systems were right in the first place?

Is the bankruptcy of Lehman Brothers only a symptom of something terribly wrong with the logic of conventional financial theories that no amount of policy intervention alone can rectify?

We are not a recently industrialized world. Nor are our financial systems stumbling with baby steps. The era of industrial revolution in the 18th and 19th century also saw the establishment of the world's first business school

'ESCP Europe' in France (1819). The modern professional accounting system originated in Scotland in the mid-nineteenth century. Several advances have been made in business management, and in financial accounting, reporting and auditing. Yet, recent history alone has witnessed three major financial crises.

The Asian financial crisis during 1993-96 had put the whole region in distress, guzzling nearly US$40 billion in rescue funds deployed by the IMF. The US sub-prime crisis eroded nearly US$29.7 trillion (46% of 2007 world market cap, 52.5% 2007 world GDP) of shareholder wealth worldwide. Another financial shock known as the 'Eurozone crisis', triggered by Greece defaulting on its huge sovereign debt, unfolded during 2010-11. More than €484 billion have since been mobilized in bailout funds from various sources. Even as the President of European Commission, Barroso, reportedly said that the worst of Europe's crisis was over, "overcoming the crisis and the crisis effects will remain a challenge over the next decade," said Weidmann, President of Germany's central bank.

History is replete with several other cases of private as well as public institutions going bankrupt, among which the US$18.5 billion bankruptcy in 2013 of Detroit - the largest US municipal bankruptcy - stands out as a sore example. Leaving aside criminal frauds, do these mishaps qualify as accidents, mistakes or errors? Particularly, in those cases involving for-profit, publicly owned business organizations.

Fraud, Accident, Mistake or Error - who is to be blamed?

Accidents are the result of flouting rules, either out of ignorance or sheer reckless disregard for them for whatever reasons. Mistake in common parlance is understood as an unintentional wrong, committed with full awareness of rules, but due to a 'mistaken' or 'misunderstood' idea about them. Is there an evil mind or a good but untrained one behind the two? Clearly, an evil mind with full understanding of rules commits well engineered frauds. The same evil mind having limited or no knowledge of rules commits accidents because it does not care for the rules. Sans the evil motive, neither a fraud nor an accident can occur, of which fraud is more condemnable than accident. Motive plays an important role in crime and punishment, and correcting the underlying evil is a difficult task. That leaves us with mistakes and errors. Both are devoid of the evil motive. That makes corrective action easier since the evil which blocks the remorse and the responsibility to correct, is absent. Of the two, who is to be held responsible for a 'mistake' and who for an 'error'? Logically, if things go wrong even when well defined rules are correctly interpreted and stringently followed, giving rise to 'errors' and not 'mistakes', then the responsibility for setting right the rules should squarely fall not on the perpetrator but on the rule maker, unlike the burden of rectifying the 'mistake' which falls on the perpetrator.

What prevents underlying basal tendencies to be whipped to surface by interested parties if their own survival feeds on the resultant froth? Fuld may not have been completely wrong in pointing out: "....it's not surprising that the media coverage of Lehman's demise has been rife with rumors and inaccuracies..." Once creating-chaos-and-feeding-on-the-froth plays out, it's not easy to stop opportunistic forces from capitalizing on it. The tendency of milking the disaster dominates the need for educating to prevent recurrence. Take for example 'TIME' which carried an article and opinion poll titled '25 People to Blame for the Financial Crisis' on their website, listing their top 25 picks including everyone from former Federal Reserve chairman Alan Greenspan and former President George W. Bush to the former CEO of Merrill Lynch and the American consumer, as well as encouraging its readers to poll for who they thought, deserved the most and the least blame.

In a free economy, it's difficult to curb opinions without the associated cost of being blamed for gagging the freedom of expression, especially that of the media. Media has a job to do - to inform. But media is human too, so is equally susceptible to human vices - predominantly 'greed', same as what prevails in financial markets, except, unlike financial markets, 'fear' is absent! Unless regulators know exactly what to regulate in the interest of investor protection, and more importantly unless investors educate themselves with financial knowledge, they will be at the mercy of the so called 'financial experts' and mostly left to fend for themselves with little success. Once a crisis occurs, it is undeniably painful for the victims, but inevitable financial bail outs put enormous stresses on the saviors too. The burden of huge amounts of money doled out in bailout funds has to be eventually borne by society when governments use public funds for the purpose.

Public companies carry the responsibility of protecting shareholder wealth. The most important role of company boards is that of diligently discharging their role as 'Agents' of shareholders, whose funds they are entrusted with. Before committing shareholders' funds into projects, diligent economic evaluation forms a critical responsibility. This calls for application of scientific principles. Post facto measurement of actual results must also be done in a scientific manner. Allowing subjectivity to creep into the process would expose decision making to various heuristic errors. Behavioral psychology has contributed significantly towards understanding the impact of cognitive errors on judgement and decision making. In this area, the 'Prospect Theory' developed by Nobel Laureate Daniel Kahneman is well known. Behavioural finance theories tell us that participants in financial markets do not make rational decisions all the time. While the vast amount of research in behavioral finance has been largely devoted to understanding the impact of cognitive errors on investor decisions, we must also examine whether the same cognitive flaws can contaminate corporate decision making! Why can't it be a case of 'Markets OK, but Companies not OK'? We might find surprises!

Should corporate financial practitioners rely on irrational short-term market behaviour for making project investment decisions in the absence of a rational asset pricing model? Do cognitive flaws that give rise to modeling errors exist in financial systems? Is Richard Fuld telling us something we don't want to hear, because we are prejudiced to believe all the right rules are already in place? Are we willing to introspect and find out whether the existing financial theories need change?

Evolution of various financial systems over the years to ensure security, transparency and stability of the economies they represent, in terms of regulatory and deterrent laws and better law enforcement, can only have a limited effect. Defining 'what to do' without a review of 'how to do' also raises investor expectations and causes greater damage if such higher expectations fail on delivery. Presence of undetected cognitive errors would impair goal setting and execution, aggravating the prospects of disappointment driven loss of shareholder value.

A systematic diagnosis of various corporate finance practices to explore the possibility of hidden cognitive flaws must break the boundaries of convention and ask fundamental questions that have never been asked before.

 **Think!**

Are the principles of corporate finance in conformity with economic rationale?

Do corporate finance practitioners 'Plan for the right goals', 'Do the right things' and 'Check against the right benchmarks' and 'Take the right Actions'?

Is risk and return correctly understood by company boards so as to discharge their agency role diligently?

2

Barricades Don't Prevent Tsunamis

Why do financial crises happen? Throw this question at anyone and one word would almost instinctively be tossed out in reply by most: 'greed', in an acquiescent tone that betrays utter helplessness; 'how could individual freedom be curbed', many would say. This would imply that goading the entire human race with the 'Ten Commandments' of virtuous behavior would be the only solution to curb the 'vice' with some hope. Don't humans suffer from other vices too? Doesn't social order put curbs and formally forbid many of them? Nothing stops someone for example, from coveting another's possession, but law forbids stealing! In contrast, while everyone knows smoking tobacco is injurious to health, it is difficult to ban the cigarette industry because smokers would protest that it violates individual freedom. Because people can't resist the urge to smoke, cigarette makers may at the most be compelled to print vivid warnings on their wares and ban adware, including surrogate advertising, in some countries. Heavy taxes may to some extent deter people from buying cigarettes. Yet, all of that may not sufficiently curb the urge as much as it expands private and public coffers. Is 'greed' operating in financial markets akin to 'theft' or 'smoking'?

Can barricades prevent Tsunamis?

In December 2013, 'The Telegraph (U.K)' reported the British drug maker GlaxoSmithKline (GSK) having stopped paying doctors to promote its drugs and delink its sales representatives' pay from the number of prescriptions written. Even though such malpractice is commonplace in the pharmaceutical industry, GSK was the first to initiate the change, reportedly triggered by a major bribery investigation in China.

What forbids financial intermediaries such as broking firms, mutual funds, and investment advisory companies from linking the incentives of their dealers to the number of client accounts and transactions? Just as patients, trusting their doctors, become gullible victims of unwarranted prescriptions, so do naïve investors to attractively designed money expanding strategies, tips and schemes, trusting not merely their direct advisors but also a host of other influencers from the financial world. Just as people recommend physicians and medicines to other people, irrational investor sentiments are fanned by other investors.

The matter doesn't end here. Just as higher drug production and sales, driven by higher prescription volume, deceptively auto-suggests patients, doctors and other drug makers about higher popularity of the drug, higher trading volumes driving stock prices higher, creates a self feeding loop. You would believe that the vicious loop would ensnare only investors. But unfortunately, as the collapse of Lehman and others illustrates, even companies rely on the same market feedback for making their project investment decisions. Just as poor knowledge about disease and medicine makes patients gullible, so does poor knowledge about finance hurts investors. One would expect that drug makers would focus their energies on understanding disease and producing appropriate preventive and curative medicines rather than be dictated by sales statistics.

Shouldn't the potency of medicine to eliminate disease gradually lead to a decline in its sales as the disease itself gets eradicated? On similar lines, do the managements of public companies, in their role as shareholders' agents, correctly understand rational shareholders' expectations and deploy equity funds optimally, or are their decisions dictated by irrational market behaviour?

Companies do not rely on shareholders' funds alone, but also take on debt. When companies borrow from commercial banks, the lending is regulated by prescribed norms and limits. Central banks define rules to curb excessive risk exposure in commercial lending. The primary purpose is to protect the banking institution, because depositors' money - a contractual liability for banks - is at stake. Stock market regulators also do the same - prescribing deposits, margins, exposure limits and trading guidelines to its members.

So what is it that makes financial markets go haywire time and again? Just as the 'statutory warning' on cigarette packs has limited effect, so does the mandatory caveats spelt out by fund managers and stock market regulators to investors.

Few would have missed repeated onslaughts of the well rehearsed monologue "Equity investments are subject to market risks. Please read the offer document carefully before investing", that accompanies every equity investment scheme announced on television or in print. The only difference that separates the warning about smoking from the latter is that specific levels of toxins which qualify as injurious are well defined for cigarettes, whereas neither market regulators nor intermediaries nor company managements really know any more about 'market risk' than - as Nobel Laureate Robert Shiller says - a 'Knightian Uncertainty'!

The problem is not so much concerning fallibility or otherwise of how stock market systems operate. Most modern markets operate with fairly sophisticated ones that are designed - as said earlier - to protect the institution. The problem lies outside it, and right inside our minds as investors, as well as in the minds of company managers, because while companies and investors are expected to mutually understand correctly what the other communicates, the reality is shockingly divergent. If it wasn't, then no large scale financial crisis would ever occur because appropriate deterrents would prevent it. How can a fire be prevented if no one knows why it starts in the first place?

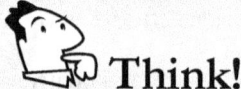

Think!

Does this not warrant delving into the causes of faulty financial practices contributing to irrational market behaviour, and eliminate them? Or should we continue to be complacent and label financial crises as 'chance', 'random', 'unpredictable' events arising from our inability to curb instinctive human greed, put up barricades around the effects while the cause remains unaddressed, and hope those barriers would withstand another financial tsunami?

Barricades Don't Prevent Tsunamis

Treading on Thin Ice

3

A Fatal Communication Error

A Fatal Communication Error

When companies deploy shareholders' funds into capital expenditure projects, they are duty bound to assess potential returns from projects against the expectations of the collective body of shareholders who form the equity market, and not that of any individual or sub-group of shareholders. The only way in which the equity market as a whole can possibly communicate its expectations to company agents - the boards - is through price behavior of the market as a whole. Market price of an individual company's stock reflects the amount investors are willing to pay to own a unit of the company's shared ownership today, so as to earn a specified expected return from future corporate earnings. Since returns from business enterprises are variable (and therefore risky), the market price too fluctuates in response to variations in current and prospective earnings announced by companies as well as estimates made by investors themselves.

Company managements must understand market expectations (implying shareholder expectations) correctly and fulfill those expectations. Shareholders assume that they do. On the other side of the fence, as is the case with warnings against smoking in a free economy, investors too are expected to understand the risks associated with business investments and behave rationally. Therefore companies assume that market prices always correctly reflect investor expectations. Both entities assuming that the behaviour of the other is right, creates a mutually feeding loop between markets and companies.

Where does the loop begin? Market price is typically indicated by the benchmark index. Does the short-term or the long-term market index correctly reflect investor expectations? Conversely, whether investors view company performance from the short-term or the long-term perspective? How would a company be able to make the right capital expenditure decisions if it does not know clearly what investors expect? Similar to the chicken-or-egg riddle, these questions have baffled financial economists worldwide for over five decades, with no clear answers available till date. Even though several theories of financial markets and related fields have been developed over the years, many of them even honored with the prestigious Nobel memorial prize, the Economic Sciences Prize Committee said in its background note "...we do not yet have complete and generally accepted explanations for how financial markets function..." even while conferring the 2013 prize for empirical research contributions towards 'Understanding Asset Prices'. The tone of the note was - we know a lot better now than before but still don't know everything!

What do we know?

The theories of asset pricing and market behavior broadly extend in two opposite directions. One dimension, the 'law of one price' or the 'Efficient Market Hypothesis' developed by Nobel Laureate Eugene Fama states that prices reflect everything, so markets are always believed to have informational efficiency. The other strand developed subsequently by Nobel Laureate Robert Shiller, based on studies in human psychology and behavior, is known as 'Behavioral Finance'. This school of thought posits that financial markets are not rational in the short term, because cognitive flaws and irrational sentiment affects investor decisions. The same school also believes that in the long term however, markets are rational. These were precisely the contributions for which the 2013 Nobel Economics Science Prize was shared by Laureates Eugene Fama, Lars Peter Hansen and Robert Shiller.

What we don't know

It goes without saying that business decisions should be based on rational logic rather than irrational sentiment. But, if financial markets are both rational and irrational in different time frames, how do we 'map' market behavior into a reasonable model that can be relied upon for decision making and fulfill investor expectations correctly? The 2013 Nobel Economic Sciences Prize Committee also confirms that as of now, no accepted asset pricing model exists.

A Fatal Communication Error

 **Think!**

Do companies and investors understand each other well or is there a mutual communication error between them that impacts rational decision making?

If their mutual communication is imperfect, what can be done to eliminate the error?

4

A Bird in Hand, or Two in the Bush?

A Bird in Hand, or Two in the Bush?

The capital asset pricing model (CAPM) was developed in 1960s to help in estimating return expectations of the equity market (typically represented by the market index). With reference to the market as a whole, expected returns of individual assets or stocks comprising the market are derived from the same model. Corporate finance prescribes that this estimate gives the representative 'Cost of Equity' and that companies must use it as a benchmark for choosing among different projects that may have disparate risk-return potential. The model has three elements. First, a reference risk free rate. Second, average returns of the market portfolio (the index). And third, an individual asset's sensitivity to market risk relative to risk of the market portfolio as a whole - known as systematic risk.

The third element is represented by 'beta (β)'. The model was built on the ideas derived from the earlier 'Modern Portfolio Theory' that explained how an ideal optimum risk-return portfolio can be constructed. Given the fact that a particular company's stock may be owned by several investors whose risk-return expectations may differ, who among the many investors represents the market? This 'base investor' or 'rational investor' was defined by the Modern Portfolio Theory, as the one who owns a well diversified portfolio (typically the stock market index), in which company specific risks - known as unsystematic risk - are cancelled out. The CAPM applies to the market portfolio held by a rational investor.

The following formula is used to estimate the cost of equity according to the Capital Asset Pricing Model.

> **Cost of Equity = Risk Free Rate + [beta * Market Risk Premium]**

'Market Risk Premium' denotes excess of long term average market return over the average benchmark interest rate of government securities.

Understanding 'market risk' and 'beta'

Systematic risk explained above refers to the risk that affects all companies in the market. For example, variations in GDP growth and inflation are common factors that affect all companies albeit in different degrees. Companies are also affected by risk arising from their own uniqueness, known as firm risk or unsystematic risk. For example, a steel making company having its own iron ore mine would not be adversely affected by increases in market prices of ore. Modern Portfolio Theory states that while unsystematic risk can be eliminated by constructing a well diversified portfolio, systematic risk cannot be diversified therefore investors expect a compensatory premium. Sensitivity to systematic risk is denoted by beta. Beta of the market portfolio is '1' and that of its components is expressed as a relative multiple to the market beta. For example if a stock is twice as sensitive to systematic risk as the market index, its 'beta' would be 2. If an asset is not correlated with the market, its beta is zero. Likewise, if an asset's return deviates in the opposite direction to the market then its beta is negative.

Companies make investments in a variety of projects. Conventional corporate financial practice prescribes that in order to estimate the expected return of a project, beta of the specific project must be applied in the CAPM model. Professional financial advisory firms regularly publish calculated betas for different industries, which may be adjusted in individual cases.

Agency role

As already mentioned, a public company's board of directors - the management - is an elected 'agent' of its shareholders. In this capacity, the management is expected to deploy shareholders' funds in a manner that the value of shareholders' investment in the company grows steadily over time. The ability to do this effectively and consistently, differentiates between exceptional, mediocre and an outright destructive management. No other resource deployed in an entrepreneurial venture would command as much premium as the quality of its management. Attempting to run a business with poor quality managerial resource would jeopardize shareholders' money invested in business, reducing managerial compensation to a bundle of wasted expenditure rather than a value creating investment in human assets.

Discharging the agency role diligently calls for the ability to make the right decisions, and to discriminate between 'reasonable risks' and 'excessive risks'. Taking 'reasonable risks' to earn 'reasonable returns', as well as rationally evaluate excess potential risks against excess potential returns, is the essence of effective performance of the 'Agency Role'. We all know the wisdom behind the proverb 'A bird in hand is worth two in a bush'. Is this not relevant for corporate decision making too?

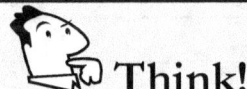 **Think!**

Who exactly is a rational investor? Is rational investor behaviour limited to eliminating only unsystematic risk through diversification? Does the same rational investor not overcome systematic risk by investing over a long term horizon? Is this equally important rational investor action overlooked while estimating market return expectations?

What exactly happens when you invest over long term? Consider Table 4-1 and the graph following it. (Figure 4-1)

Table: 4-1: Impact of 50% Fall at the End of Various Periods

Annual Average Return %	Base Period Investment	Number of Years	Terminal Value of Initial Investment
1.12	100	25	1700
1.09	100	25	850
1.12	100	20	965
1.08	100	20	482
1.12	100	15	547
1.07	100	15	274
1.12	100	10	311
1.04	100	10	155
1.12	100	5	176
0.98	100	5	88

The above table shows how much an initial investment of 100 would compound to over various periods given an annual average return of 12%. For each period, the second line shows the effect of a 50% fall in the terminal value, and the corresponding impact on annual average rate of return. As the investment period shortens, a 50% fall at the end of the period translates to a decreasing annual average return for the corresponding period. Figure 4-1 shows a graphical representation of the phenomenon. Clearly, all things being constant, each five year drop in investment period has caused the annual average to fall at an increasing rate, seen in the downward curving graph. If the average inflation was say 6%, then for investment periods below 15 years, real returns are negative - worst for 5 years where even the initial investment has been eroded, whereas for higher periods, average returns have beaten inflation. Adding to this, since the short-term has greater exposure to extreme variations in returns (volatility), the chances of achieving the average 12% return further reduces. In contrast, longer periods automatically render short term volatility irrelevant, increasing the changes of achieving the long term average return.

Figure 4-1: Impact of 50% Fall at the End of Various Periods

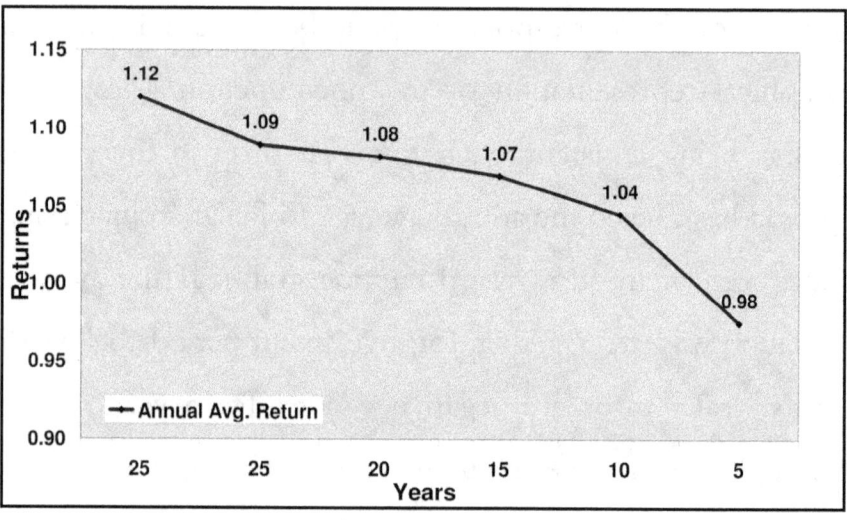

A related question that must be raised is: Is the practice of applying project specific beta for evaluating capital expenditure projects, as prescribed by corporate finance, in conformity with well established economic principles which are applied in other areas of finance and economics such as the concepts of 'marginal' and 'opportunity cost'?

No matter what company managements do, the only options available to investors are either to continue to hold their current investment in the company or modify/sell-off their stake. This implies that investors would evaluate the marginal impact of specific company actions on the company as a whole. The stand-alone risk or opportunity of any one project in isolation cannot be a relevant benchmark for investors, because what matters to them is 'total company returns'. Applying 'project beta' in the CAPM to determine criterion cost of equity during project evaluation clearly conflicts with this goal leading to crucial investment decisions going wrong.

This has a direct bearing on the effective performance of 'agency role'. Erroneous methods being followed adversely impact the 'agency cost' arising either due to investments being made in high risk projects or when profitable, reasonable-risk investments are rejected. When companies invest in high-risk high-return projects based on faulty evaluation tools about which investors are not aware of, it signals a false sense of optimism in financial markets, contributing to irrational euphoria and inevitable crashes in financial markets if expected returns do not fructify.

5

Missing the Opportunity Cost

Treading on Thin Ice

Although the CAPM developed in the 1960s appears fairly straightforward, several anomalies soon surfaced in the model, spurring thousands of studies, but all of them failed to establish the model's validity. Despite its defects, the CAPM remains a widely practiced and taught model worldwide in the absence of an alternative. In its background note, the 2013 Nobel Economic Sciences Prize Committee reports:

"Shiller argued that stock prices are particularly vulnerable to psychological biases because of the ambiguity in the true value of a stock, due to the lack of an accepted valuation model (i.e., investors face "Knightian uncertainty" rather than risk)."

Even the recent good practice guidance published by International Federation of Accountants (IFAC), an apex international standard setting body, highlights the unreliability of this very foundation on which shareholder value creation rests. The classical CAPM model and few examples of the arguments against it are shown below.

> **The Capital Asset Pricing Model (CAPM)**
> **Cost of Equity = Risk Free Rate + [beta x Market Risk Premium]**

"One More Caveat Regarding the CAPM Approach: We should point out one more potential problem with the CAPM: It has never been proven that investors base their required rates of return on the equation $r_M = r_{RF} + (RP_M)$ bi. Hundreds, perhaps thousands of studies have been conducted to test the validity of the CAPM, but there have been no definitive answers." – Source: p-352, 'Corporate Finance: A Focused Approach', 4th edition, Michael C. Ehrhardt, University of Tennessee and Eugene F. Brigham, University of Florida, South-Western Cengage Learning.

*"**Some Final Observations:** ....We recognize that the market equilibrium process is complex and that CAPM cannot give a precise measurement of the required return for a particular company. Still the CAPM trade-off between risk and return is a useful guide for approximating capital costs and thereby allocating capital to investment projects"* - Source: p-74, Financial Management & Policy, 12th edition, James C Van Horne, Stanford University, Pearson Education Asia

'International Good Practice Guidance' on 'Project & Investment Appraisal for Sustainable Value Creation' issued by IFAC in Aug 2013

"Para B3 - The cost of capital associated with investment and capital budgeting decisions is the weighted average cost of capital (WACC). Determining the cost of equity capital can be particularly difficult, as the application of techniques such as the Capital Asset Pricing Model (CAPM) can be complex, and subject to a number of challenges and limitations"

"Para B5. The application of CAPM as a measure of risk can be particularly problematic as it is based on portfolio theory, which assumes that markets are efficiently priced to reflect greater return for greater risk, and that investors are perfectly diversified. Although

CAPM might be used as a basis of understanding the relationship between expected risk and expected return, the assumptions upon which it is based should be understood and challenged"

The model is expressed as a regression equation as shown below:

Ri = Rf + b (Rm − Rf)

Where:
Ri = Return from asset 'i' comprising the market portfolio
Rf = Average return from risk free asset 'f' (benchmark interest rate)
Rm = Average long term returns from market portfolio 'm'
b = Beta coefficient [Covariance (Ri, Rm) ÷ Variance(Rm)]
Rm − Rf = Average market risk premium

In simple words the model expresses the estimated return of an asset (Ri) as a sum of risk-free rate (Rf) and a risk premium (Rm - Rf) which varies depending on the asset's beta.

Various empirical studies carried out to test the model showed that the intercept **'Rf'** (representing the riskless rate of return) implied from the test results was much larger than the actual risk-free rate, so there is an unexplained gap in the equation. That is to say:

If **Ri = Rf + [b (Rm − Rf)]** was true,

then **Rf** should be equal to **Ri − [b (Rm − Rf)]**

However when **Ri − [b (Rm − Rf)]** was substituted with actual figures, the resultant **'Rf'** was implausibly greater than actual **'Rf'**. There was a missing term **[x]** as shown below.

Ri = Rf + [b (Rm − Rf)] + [x]

What is the flaw?

Fundamental flaws in the CAPM are two. First, it uses the benchmark interest rate as a reference 'risk free' return (Rf) which conflicts with economic reasoning. Economic science tells us that 'interest' is principally a compensation for inflation, setting aside other influencing factors. No entrepreneur would find any economic activity worthwhile if the prospective returns (opportunity cost) from entrepreneurship merely compensates for inflation. Some reward for entrepreneurial effort must also form the opportunity cost. Second, even though beta is a measure of relative risk, and risk is correctly measured by deviations from mean, the model applies beta to a measure of mean, which market risk premium (MRP) truly is, instead of applying it to deviations in MRP. In fact the model does not account for deviations in market risk premium at all. On the contrary it considers the average market risk premium itself as a proxy for market risk. If market risk premium represents compensation for risk, then what is the reward and the opportunity cost of entrepreneurial efforts? In particular, think of the case where beta is 'zero' or 'negative'! Zero beta would make the cost of equity equal to the benchmark interest rate implying that for a business whose returns are not correlated with the market (which zero beta implies), the returns expected by entrepreneurs would be same as the benchmark interest rate, which is absurd. When beta is negative (implying that returns from the asset varies in the opposite direction to the market), expected equity returns would turn out to be lower than the benchmark interest rate - an even greater absurdity.

The rationale put forward by the model
For using the benchmark interest rate on government securities as the proxy for the risk-free return (Rf), the CAPM forwards the argument that any investor (such as an entrepreneur or equity shareholder) who owns risky assets (such as business firms or equity shares of public companies) would desire at least as much rate of return from such investments as would have been otherwise earned from the same funds invested 'risk-free' elsewhere. In other words interest rate is considered as the risk-free 'opportunity cost' of funds.

Opportunity cost represents the returns forgone from another similar activity. How can the opportunity cost of 'entrepreneurial activity' be based on returns forgone from 'doing nothing' but passively invest in interest bearing government securities that primarily only compensate inflation?

Further, the rationale put forward for 'Market Risk Premium' (Rm - Rf) is that it represents the extra return an entrepreneur must earn from business as a compensation for entrepreneurial risk. Equity investors are de-facto entrepreneurs because they are the owners of businesses. Since long-term average returns from the market portfolio (typically an equity index) is represented by 'Rm', the term (Rm - Rf) constitutes the 'excess' or the 'premium' for risk.

If benchmark interest rate is deemed to be the correct risk-free reference, what would be the risk-free opportunity cost in a situation where interest rates are close to zero because inflation is near zero?

Would two markets otherwise similar in all respects, be considered equal in risk-return characteristics if their average market risk premia over time are equal, even if the periodic variations in premia differ? Obviously the one with greater variation would be riskier. However, when the CAPM is applied, both would produce the same cost of equity for the market portfolio because beta would be '1' in either case.

Missing the Opportunity Cost

Would the uncertain opportunity of gains in excess of benchmark interest rate (and the equally uncertain risk of earning lower than interest), constitute the reward for entrepreneurial 'efforts' or is it the average premium? In the above example, investors should be indifferent between the two markets if only the long-term and the associated average market return are relevant (because in that case short-term variation in returns becomes irrelevant). This should be true for a rational investor who invests only for the long term. Therefore what is the relevance of short-term variations and its measure - beta? Since beta is a measure of systematic risk (variation in returns), but variations turn out to be irrelevant for the long term for a rational investor, it renders beta irrelevant. Yet the CAPM uses beta for estimating cost of equity, which makes it questionable.

Further, variations between 'average annual returns' during the life of the project (not annual variations) vis-à-vis the 'long term average expected return' would still be relevant for the project as a whole. Therefore the question arises: How to estimate this variance and whether beta should be applied to this it instead of the average market risk premium as prescribed by the CAPM? The appropriate statistical tool for measuring this variance is the 'standard error of sampling distribution'. Detailed explanation of sampling distribution and its relevance for asset pricing is beyond the scope of this book. Interested readers may refer to the book 'The Timeless Essence of Financial Science', for details.

 **Think!**

Unless company managements correctly understand and define shareholder expectations, that is, the opportunity cost of equity, would they be able to deliver the expected returns?

Missing the Opportunity Cost

6

Fooled by the Mean

Conventionally, in corporate finance practice, beta adjusted cost of equity derived from the CAPM is applied as a discounting rate to convert annual estimated future cash flows from a equity funded capital investment project into a consolidated present value. The method is known as 'Discounted Cash Flow' (DCF) method. It fundamentally uses the financial concept of 'Time Value of Money'. The 'time value' is based on the idea that a dollar received in future is less valuable than a dollar received today. This is because of two principal factors which erode its purchasing power. First is inflation. If prices of goods and services in an economy increase, then the dollar received in future would be able to buy less than what it can buy now. Second, even if there is a possibility of receiving more than a dollar in future, the outcome could be uncertain. We may even lose some money and actually receive less than a dollar or even zero! In short, there is risk involved. Conventional financial practice prescribes that all future cash flows should be discounted - thus converted to present value - at an appropriate 'risk adjusted' rate. This brings all cash inflows and outflows to a common comparable point in time that is 'now'. The net result of present values of cash inflows and outflows is called 'Net Present Value' (NPV). Projects that produce positive NPV are considered investment worthy, while others are not. When multiple projects are simultaneously evaluated, they are ranked on the basis of a 'Profitability Index' (PI) which is nothing but a ratio: PV of inflows / PV of outflows.

The method described above has been followed worldwide for decades, a fact confirmed by the findings of a survey by the Association For Financial Professionals (AFP) reported in Harvard Business Review, July 2012, titled "Do You Know Your Cost of Capital?" The relevant extract from this report is reproduced below.

> "……80% of more than 300 respondents – of which 90% with over $ 1 billion in revenues – use free-cash-flow projections discounted by the weighted average of the costs of debt and equity, to estimate the value of investments.
>
> ……about 90% of the respondents use the capital assets pricing model (CAPM), which quantifies the return required by an investment on the basis of the associated risk."

The method is believed to squeeze 'more bang for the buck' from every investment, and advocated as such in all professional Post Graduate Business Management programs taught worldwide. See examples below.

"The profitability index was designed to select the projects with the most bang per buck—the greatest NPV per dollar spent. That's the right objective when bucks are limited. When they are not, a bigger bang is always better than a smaller one, even when more bucks are spent."

- Source: 'Fundamentals of Corporate Finance, 3rd edition, ISBN 0-07-553109-7, page 367. McGraw-Hill Primis

Custom Publishing, containing contributions by Richard A. Brealey, Bank of England and London Business School, Stewart C. Myers, Sloan School of Management, Massachusetts Institute of Technology, Alan J. Marcus, Wallace E. Carroll School of Management, Boston College, Stephen A. Ross, Massachusetts Institute of Technology, Randolph W. Westerfield, University of Southern California, and Bradford D. Jordan, University of Kentucky.

"....while interest rates are great at measuring "bang per buck invested," they don't measure how many bucks are being invested. More formally, this is described as a problem concerning differences in scale between projects"
- Source: 'Corporate Finance Demystified – A Self Teaching Guide', ISBN: 0-07-145910-3, page 133, McGraw-Hill, Troy A. Adair, Jr. Ph.D. University of Michigan.

The crux is in cash flows, which the fallacy of mean hides.

All elements of risk involved in an investment project, ultimately manifest as cash flow disruptions. Failure to understand this aspect of capital budgeting well and manage it effectively makes the difference between a smoothly functioning enterprise steadily creating value for its shareholders, and a crippling liquidity crunch that could spiral out of control into bankruptcy.

If cash flows of all periods are consolidated into a single present value, how does a business entity identify periodic adverse cash flow deviations? Unless cash flows of each period are measured against an appropriate periodic benchmark, how would it be possible to say whether or not an adverse cash flow in any particular period constitutes risk? It could well be a harmless minor deviation! The principle of management by exception would be impossible to apply unless managers are able to first define what constitutes normal cash flows, and then assess whether or not a specific negative deviation is large enough to jeopardize the overall returns of the project as a whole, or is only a minor harmless one.

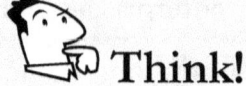 **Think!**

Doesn't the present corporate financial practice of consolidating all cash flows into a single point, only provide information about the average returns on the project as a whole and not tell anything about periodic cash flow fluctuations? Would this not expose projects to unforeseen liquidity crisis and consequently hurt shareholders' expectations?

Fooled by the Mean

7

WACC

a Fallacy!

Like the CAPM, the Weighted Average Cost of Capital (WACC) is also widely used globally for evaluating capital expenditure projects as well as for determination of enterprise value. While the CAPM derived cost of equity is applied in discounting pure equity funded projects, WACC is used where projects are financed from multiple sources, most commonly various proportions of debt and equity. WACC came into practice when the theory of 'one value' was introduced around the same time as the CAPM. In simple words, the 'one-value' theory stated that two firms alike in every respect except capital structure must have the same total value. If not, arbitrage will drive their values together. In fact the CAPM determined cost of equity forms one of the components in WACC. The popularity of

WACC is also evident in the findings of the same research mentioned earlier, which was published in the Harvard Business Review titled "Do You Know Your Cost of Capital?" (see extract below).

> *"......80% of more than 300 respondents – of which 90% with over $ 1 billion in revenues – use free-cash-flow projections discounted by the weighted average of the costs of debt and equity, to estimate the value of investments........about 90% of the respondents use the capital assets pricing model (CAPM), which quantifies the return required by an investment on the basis of the associated risk."*

The central idea behind WACC is that any capital investment project must earn a return that exceeds its average financing cost. If projects are funded by multiple sources of capital, average cost must be determined by applying the proportions of each source as weights. Weights are determined on the basis of market value of each source. The resultant WACC is then applied as the appropriate discounting factor for converting all cash flows to a single present value. The evaluation assumes that returns are compounded; hence intermediate cash flows are deemed to be reinvested at the WACC rate.

How does 'cost-of-capital' compare with costs of other factors of production?

Economic science tells us that the entrepreneur is a catalyst who drives other factors of production towards the desired output. Each factor seeks a reward. Land requires rent, labour expects wages and interest must be paid for borrowed capital. The opportunity cost of each factor determines its minimum reward. What is the opportunity cost of 'entrepreneurship'? Obviously 'profit'. A public company is owned by large number of shareholders including promoters. It must therefore earn at least as much profit that could have been otherwise earned by shareholders from alternate comparable use of equity funds. However, the inherent characteristic of entrepreneurship embodies an important feature, that is, the reward for entrepreneurship cannot be enjoyed unless all other factors have been paid for, including interest payments on borrowed capital.

How do other economic agents view entrepreneurial profits?

'Company Law' by whatever name called in different countries, views a company as a collective entrepreneurial venture, bearing a distinct identity as an artificial judicial person. The obligations of companies – and implicitly, that of its owners - towards external entities, are well defined for all mutual commercial transactions between them. Without fulfilling these obligations, profit cannot be determined. 'Income Tax laws' consider 'interest on borrowings' as an expense, deductable for determination of profits. 'Accounting and reporting' rules make a distinction between owners' equity and other liabilities, and are aligned with company law. All of the aforesaid elements recognize owners' funds as risk capital. All of them also consider profits as residual reward left over after the rewards for all other factors, including borrowed capital are paid.

How do rating agencies view borrowings?

A verbatim extract from Standard & Poor's ratings definitions reproduced below gives a general idea of how entities are assessed for risk. Primarily risk here refers to the risk of default in meeting debt obligations. Though the ratings are classified into various categories, the general principles are same for all.

"Credit ratings are forward-looking opinions about credit risk. Standard & Poor's credit ratings express our opinion about the ability and willingness of an issuer, such as a corporation or state or city government, to meet its financial obligations in full - and on time."

It is clear from above that only residual cash flows are available to equity. If cash flows are inadequate to fulfill debt obligations, it would precipitate a liquidity crunch, and in the worst case, bankruptcy. Rating agencies evaluate debt issuers based on their ability to service debt, whether short term or long term.

>  **Think!**
>
> Is the practice of putting debt and equity together in WACC while selecting projects, consistent with the fact that debt does not share risk, but enjoys priority for receiving rewards and repayment of principal? For determining WACC, is it appropriate to apply market value as weights? Does that not create unwarranted distortion in cost of equity?

A company with a consistently good financial performance would be viewed with optimism by the equity market and enjoy good demand for its shares. Therefore its market price is likely to be high. Behavioural finance tells us that market prices are driven by irrational euphoria or panic in the short term. This would lead to two effects. One, the beta of good performers is likely to be high in the short term because their stock price would outperform the market resulting in a higher CAPM derived cost of equity. Second, the high market value would increase the market value weightage applied to determine WACC, resulting in an absurd outcome of high cost of capital for a consistently good performing company. The reverse phenomenon would occur for a poor performing company. Underperformance of its stock relative to the market and poor valuation would produce a low cost of capital. When these distorted costs are applied for project selection, good performers would end up rejecting otherwise profitable projects because of the abnormally high criterion cost given by WACC. Similarly poor performing companies would end up possibly accepting low return projects because the criterion cost is too low. Both cases would adversely affect shareholder value.

 **Think!**

What is the rationale for assuming that all intermediate cash flows are re-invested at the WACC, when in reality only those intermediate inflows left over after fulfilling debt obligations are available for reinvestment, not necessarily at WACC?

No two projects could be same, nor would returns over different periods be constant even for a single project. Yet, shareholders would expect that the minimum opportunity cost of equity must be earned at all times. The reinvestment assumption in corporate financial practice stated above does not take this into account. The result: distorted cash flow planning and contribution to unforeseen liquidity crisis!

Mind the Leverage!

Treading on Thin Ice

Mind the Leverage!

What's the true value of a business enterprise? For the owners of any asset, what matters is the exchange value that the asset commands in the market. A mansion of $100 million market value would fetch only $20 million to the owner if it carries a $80 million debt burden. For a new buyer of the mansion who settles the debt directly and pays the rest of the amount to the owner, its value would $100 million, whereas if the buyer decides to assume the existing debt, the property would be worth only $20 million to him. In every situation, only the net value turns out to be relevant to the owner. The market value of $100 million is meaningless to owners, except for the leverage effect of debt. That is to say, a 10% increase in market value would cause more than 10% rise in the residual value to the owner. A similar degree of fall in market value would cause a more than proportionate damage. Conversely, any change in market value would be of no significance to the lender since his claim would always be constant, defined by the contractual amount owed to him regardless of what the total market value is, and regardless of whether or not the asset has any market value at all. In extreme erosion of value, lenders would simply compel the owners to bring in fresh equity to pay off debts.

In common parlance, the term 'value' is used to describe the worth of something. It could be a tangible asset or even an intangible human quality or talent. It's no different in the commercial world, where only shareholder value gets affected by variations in business performance. When companies perform poorly, only shareholder value bears the brunt. Lenders remain fairly protected by law, and wield the power to invoke contractual clauses to recover dues, attach assets, and even gain control over the enterprises of defaulting borrowers. Doesn't the following simple meaning of value found in the Oxford dictionary best describe it, than a blind pursuit for complex models assuming that more precision would only come from greater complexity?

> *Value (n): 1. worth: desirability or utility or the qualities on which these depend; 2. amount for which a thing can be exchanged in the open market.*

Value is relative

Equity value is not an absolute but rather a relative phenomenon; the manifestation of actual or perceived corporate performance matched against shareholders' expectations. It is also a long term phenomenon. Benjamin Graham, the British-born American economist aptly described it in the following words:

"in the short term, the stock market behaves like a voting machine, but in the long term it acts like a weighing machine (i.e. its true value will in the long run be reflected in its stock price)"

Long term value could be viewed as the evolutionary end, and the short term fluctuations, as the evidence of the evolutionary process at work. Would it be possible to conceive long term market value unless short term price swings define its boundaries? Conversely, would it be possible for short term price to fluctuate without a rational pivotal point around which to swing? The following descriptions found in 'Wikipedia' aptly describes the concepts.

Value investing

"Graham's favorite allegory is that of Mr. Market, an obliging fellow who turns up every day at the shareholder's door offering to buy or sell his shares at a different price. Often, the price quoted by Mr. Market seems plausible, but sometimes it is ridiculous. The investor is free to either agree with his quoted price and trade with him, or ignore him completely. Mr. Market doesn't mind this, and will be back the following day to quote another price.

The point of this anecdote is that the investor should not regard the whims of Mr. Market as a determining factor in the value of the shares the investor owns. He should profit from market folly rather than participate in it. The investor is advised to concentrate on the real life performance of his companies and receiving dividends, rather than be too concerned with Mr. Market's often irrational behavior."

Modern Portfolio Theory

"In recent years, Graham's "Mr. Market" approach has been challenged by Modern Portfolio Theory (MPT), which is based on the hypothesis of efficiency of financial markets. A popular proponent of MPT is, for example, William J. Bernstein, whose book The Intelligent Asset Allocator extends Graham's The Intelligent Investor via an appreciation of long-term trends and the near impossibility of understanding the market at large. Modern Portfolio Theory, which is widely taught in American and British business schools, posits that it is generally impossible for any individual to consistently outwit the market, thus denying the possibility of any distinction between "market price" and "value" of a security."

Behavioral economics

"Behavioral economics and the related field, behavioral finance, study the effects of social, cognitive, and emotional factors on the economic decisions of individuals and institutions and the consequences for market prices, returns, and the resource allocation. The fields are primarily concerned with the bounds of rationality of economic agents. Behavioral models typically integrate insights from psychology with neo-classical economic theory; in so doing, these behavioral models cover a range of concepts, methods, and fields.

The study of behavioral economics includes how market decisions are made and the mechanisms that drive public choice, such as biases towards promoting self-interest.

There are three prevalent themes in behavioral finances:
- *Heuristics: People often make decisions based on approximate rules of thumb and not strict logic.*
- *Framing: The collection of anecdotes and stereotypes that make up the mental emotional filters individuals rely on to understand and respond to events.*
- *Market inefficiencies: These include mis-pricings and non-rational decision making."*

The fallacy of 'leverage adjusted beta'

The fact that financial leverage influences beta is in itself a validation that only residual value to equity matters, because 'beta' is a term associated with equities. Changes in leverage affects predisposition to systematic risk, therefore beta, and through it, the cost of equity as given by the CAPM. 'Beta' based on historical data serves limited purpose if subsequent changes take place in the capital structure, altering the risk to equity. In corporate financial practice, conventionally, historical 'beta' is calibrated to different proportions of debt and equity. This is called leverage adjusted beta. The following formula is applied for achieving this objective.

New beta = old beta / [1 + (1-t) old D/E] x [1 + (1-t) new D/E]

(Where D/E =debt / equity ratio and, 't' =income tax rate)
(Source: 'Adjusting the Beta for Leverage', James C. Van Horne, Stanford University, Financial Management & Policy, 12th edition, pp 207-208)

Beta reflects the degree of systematic risk that equity is exposed to. Given a certain amount of total capital, the quantum and variation in net operating profits available to equity - which has an impact on equity value - depends on four factors.

a) Total amount of operating profits before interest
b) Proportion of debt and equity
c) Interest rate on debt
d) Corporate income tax rate

However, the above formula takes into account only two elements, (b) the debt-equity ratio and (d) the corporate income tax rate. It ignores (a) total income and (c) interest rate of debt, both being important determinants of residual income which consequently affects equity value.

Tweaking any model with D/E adjustments alone cannot result in better risk management. On the contrary, it would only amount to faulty diagnosis and faulty treatment. Shouldn't risk and return management therefore pay attention to the cash flow impact and not merely the capital structure?

The risk of leverage is well known to equity investors, and prudent investment management always discourages investors against excessive leverage. Yet, large number of investors, which includes certain types of mutual funds, do indulge in leveraging their investment.

Having said that, do ordinary equity investors really understand whether the companies they invest in are rational in their leveraging decisions? How careful are company managements about ensuring that excessive

Mind the Leverage!

leverage does not hurt shareholder wealth? Rampant, reckless leveraging ends up eroding not only shareholders' capital but also causes damage to the banking systems when billions are written off in losses from non-performing assets because companies cannot fulfill their debt obligations.

 **Think!**

When higher leverage increases the predisposition of equity to systematic risk, driving up 'beta' and thus 'cost of equity', what is the rationale in believing that simply raising the cost of equity in tandem with the higher beta and using the resultant higher cost as the criterion for project selection would mitigate the inherent risk and produce the desired higher returns?

If risk-return management was as simple as raising the bar of criterion cost of capital, then no asset pricing model would be required in the first place! Arbitrarily inflating the calculated cost of capital by a few points for various factors is a common corporate finance practice! And there is plenty of evidence of companies facing financial stress, going bankrupt, and billions of corporate loans written off by banks. The brunt of this is borne by ordinary shareholders because the market price of such companies would plummet. Promoter shareholders' stake is not traded on the stock exchanges. Even if the market price of their stake is also indirectly affected, does it really matter? In their capacity as members of the management board, promoters receive generous amounts in salaries and perquisites, which could more than make up the losses in their equity stake and ensure a good return on investment on their stake!

Excessive leverage undertaken by companies creates irrational optimism if the markets are attracted by prospective high returns and overlook the risks. This may happen because of a false sense of confidence that may be sent out when companies borrow big for various seemingly attractive projects, particularly when market sentiment is already bullish. Markets have no way to know whether company managements follow scientific methods for deploying shareholders' funds or may assume that they do!

Mind the Leverage!

Is Budgeting Aligned to Value Creation?

Is Budgeting Aligned to Value Creation?

Markets are rational in the long term. There's ample evidence in support of this. Therefore 'good management practice' must take a long-term perspective while making financial decisions and not blindly use methods that rely on inevitable short-term variations. Successful business leaders and the enterprises they lead, have achieved excellence only by consciously practicing and promoting the pursuit of long-term goals. Yet, the long-term goal cannot be achieved without surviving short-term risks. The currently practiced Discounted Cash Flow (DCF) method, where future streams of project cash flows are consolidated into a single Net Present Value (NPV) overlooks the risk arising from periodic variations in cash flows. Also the fact that debt obligations are not accounted for as cash flows despite having a cash flow impact, and as explained earlier, the cost of debt being wrongly consolidated into WACC, compounds the problem.

From an economic value creation perspective, the relationship between i) operating profits, ii) cost of debt, iii) cost of equity and iv) economic value is essentially a sequential, inter-dependent structure, precisely in that order. We can say that operating profits (−) cost of debt = gross residual income and gross residual income (−) cost of equity = net residual income or economic value added. This structure is in perfect alignment with the economic reality that entrepreneurial reward of profit constitutes residual income after all other factors of production have been paid out. The excess amount left over after deducting opportunity cost of equity represents the true economic value added for the entrepreneur or the equity investor.

Aligning methods with goals

Conventional capital budgeting procedure continues to use WACC as the criterion cost to discount pre-interest cash profits. While the goal of corporate finance is to protect and enhance shareholder value, this purpose is defeated because the decision making method is misaligned with the goal. While the goal is to enhance post interest residual income which benefits shareholders, the method consolidates interest cost and cost of equity into a common cost of capital. One article titled 'Framework For Financial Decisions' which appeared in the Harvard Business Review March 1971 issue, only a few years after both CAPM and WACC were introduced in corporate financial practice, precisely articulates the ambiguity in decision making that existed then - and to a large extent even now. The article remarked:

> *"It is up to the corporate financial officers to determine **this relationship** and project its likely future. Their judgments are aided by keeping in touch with the company's professional advisers in the financial markets".*

The 'relationship' was a reference to the link between 'Price/Earnings Ratio' – an aspect of valuation, and 'Debt/Equity Ratio' – an aspect of capital structure. If the 'advisors in the financial markets' should be looked up to for expertise, where would the advisors look for guidance?

Wouldn't lack of robust official guidelines render decision making subjective?

Capital budgeting procedure must align with economic reality, draw attention to the effect of leverage risk on cash flows, and prevent unforeseen liquidity crisis from causing erosion of shareholder value. Only then, enterprise managements would be able to discharge the agency role diligently. Performing the agency role well calls for minimizing the two agency costs: one arising from wrongly rejecting otherwise profitable projects based on negative NPV arising from erroneously high criterion cost of capital, and the other arising from wrongly accepting sub-optimal return projects based on positive NPV arising from erroneously low cost of capital. Company managements must use the correct criterion cost of capital so as to deliver the minimum expected opportunity cost of equity to shareholders first, and then evaluate excess prospective returns against associated excess risks. However, current capital budgeting methods are not in sync with this goal, because interest cost is not considered as a component of cash flows in DCF based capital budgeting.

Many organizations choose not to use DCF methods for project evaluation and follow the non-DCF route instead - such as the Pay Back Period (PBP) method; and the list includes even well known multinational companies. Non-DCF methods are mere routes of convenience and lack economic rationale. This fact has also been emphatically highlighted in the 'International Good Practice Guidance' on 'Project & Investment Appraisal for Sustainable Value Creation' issued by IFAC in Aug 2013. It says:

"Organizations with explicit sustainable value-creating strategies typically emphasize techniques such as DCF and real options and downplay the role of other short-term measurement criteria, such as payback and earnings per share (EPS) growth. Research shows that a significant number of organizations do not prioritize such techniques when perhaps they should, especially in assessing strategic investment decisions and taking a long-term view. This applies to smaller organizations where their use of such techniques is particularly variable as many rely on relatively simple approaches, such as payback criteria and informal rules of thumb. More sophisticated approaches are needed where a decision is large relative to the business and covers a longer term than most of the organization's decisions"

Conventional payback period method (PBP) takes into account undiscounted cash flows. Projects are accepted if the initial investment is fully recovered through cash flows within a specified target period. As a result, any risk arising from cash flows diminishing beyond the payback period is ignored. There is an implied hope in this method that the already recovered initial amount will be redeployed profitably. In the event that adverse economic conditions may threaten future cash flows from the current project, how can the success of finding new profitable projects be guaranteed? In such a situation, the likelihood of debt defaults in future would also remain intact if the projects are funded through borrowings. In addition, higher initial cash flows may also create undue euphoria in financial markets and raise equity valuations, setting the stage for abnormal damage to equity value if actual cash flows fall short and debt defaults occur subsequently.

A variation of payback period method, using discounted cash flows is also practiced. Except for producing an extended payback period, the cash flow risk still remains. In either case unforeseen losses beyond the pay back period may wipe out previous gains. PBP is also unsuitable where investment outflows are staggered over multiple periods.

> 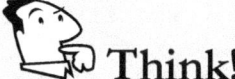 **Think!**
>
> **If the capital budgeting process is not aligned with residual-profit-to-equity principle, how can it achieve the twin objectives of delivering reasonable returns with reasonable risks, and evaluate excess returns against excess risks? How would company managements be able to discharge the agency role?**

What would be a prudent choice given two projects, one providing high initial cash flows followed by rapidly diminishing subsequent flows and another producing stable cash flows throughout project life? Wouldn't rational investors prefer the latter?

10

Is Value Creation Correctly Measured?

Treading on Thin Ice

Is Value Creation Correctly Measured?

Capital clings to value like iron filings to a magnet, and scatters equally fast when there's nothing to attract it. 'Value' has been a matter of great discussion among economists and is linked to price through the mechanism of exchange between buyer and sellers. Buyers express what they are willing to pay for acquiring assets, whereas sellers, what compensation they are willing to accept in exchange for giving up ownership of those assets. Whether a publicly owned asset such as a business enterprise has created or destroyed value is ultimately reflected in its long term stock price. The stock market not only reacts to actual performance of these enterprises, thereby impacting their value, but also responds to various actions taken by their managements, judging their effect on future value. The undisputable truth is that investors want to acquire assets today at a price they consider commensurate with the estimated future value creating capability of the assets.

Historical value accretion acts as a buffer that absorbs future value impairment. Any measurement of value should therefore objectively address two key questions. Whether value has been already created and accumulated and whether future value nurturing actions are being currently taken. Market prices do reflect the collective opinion of different players in different timeframes and substantial element of speculation is present in short term prices. Shouldn't corporate finance focus on enhancing long term value?

Value creation in a business enterprise is achieved when its financial resources are utilized wisely. This must essentially involve application of fundamentally sound economic rationale and following well structured steps across the entire Plan-Do-Check-Act cycle that forms the core of any strategic management process. All steps in the PDCA cycle must align with the 'Value Creation' goal, be consistent with each other and follow a common thread.

The quest for managerial excellence has led to the development of several 'performance evaluation tools', ranging from simple ratio analysis to strategy tools like the Balanced-Score-Card, Hoshin-Kanri, EVA®, as well as various attempts to expand the measurement of 'Value', integrating non-financial parameters into it. Whatever tool is used to measure performance, in the ultimate analysis, it should correctly measure whether the business is adding shareholder value or not.

Analysing EVA ®

One tool that gained popularity for value measurement is Economic Value Added (EVA®). Essentially a variation of Residual Income Valuation of economic profit, EVA makes several adjustments to the reported operating profit before using it in the calculation. Following is a verbatim reproduction about EVA® from www.sternstewart.com, the management consulting firm which created and owns this metric.

"Economic Value Added is a measure of economic profit. It is calculated as the difference between the Net Operating Profit After Tax and the opportunity cost of invested Capital. This opportunity cost is determined by the weighted average cost of Debt and Equity Capital ("WACC") and the amount of Capital employed. An equivalent way to calculate EVA® is to multiply Capital by the difference between the Return on Capital and the WACC. If one of the firm's goals is to increase EVA® on a sustainable basis, notice from this formula that it can be accomplished in four different ways. First, the firm can grow the business by investing where the returns exceed the WACC. Second, the firm can improve the operating efficiencies on its existing Capital, thereby increasing the return on Capital. Third, a firm can harvest Capital from its losing investments, where the return is less than the WACC and has almost no hope for improving. The funds thus generated by harvesting are disgorged to the shareholders or it is used to make worthwhile investments elsewhere. Fourth, the firm can increase its ratio of debt-to-equity when doing so lowers the WACC and doesn't threaten flexibility or survival.

What separates EVA® from other performance metrics such as EPS, EBITDA, and ROIC is that it measures all of the costs of running a business-operating and financing. This makes EVA® the soundest performance metric and the one most closely aligned with the creation of shareholder value. In fact, EVA® and Net Present Value arithmetically tie, so companies can be assured that increasing EVA® is always a good thing for its investors - certainly not the case with EPS (see Enron) or Free Cash Flow. Many even argue that EVA® is a better decision tool than NPV because it captures the period-by-period value creation or destruction of a given firm or investment, and makes it easy to audit performance against management projections.

Given the usefulness of the measure, many companies have adopted it as part of a comprehensive management and incentive system that drives their decision processes. Such focus on value creation has served the shareholders of these companies well. Between 1997 and 2007, Stern Stewart & Co.'s EVA® adopters have beat broader market indices by a significant margin"

Does EVA® adequately measure value?

Value creation is essentially a long term process and the result of strategic decisions and actions. These decisions and actions relate to three key areas - investment, financing and operations.

The formula for calculating EVA:

EVA = net operating profit after taxes – a capital charge

$$[NOPAT - (WACC \times Capital)]$$

Alternatively,

$$EVA = (r - WACC) \times capital$$

Where r = operating rate of return

Although EVA was developed to improve over the older Residual Income Valuation method, it suffers from certain fundamental weaknesses in its interpretation of 'Value' itself as discussed below.

a) Universally, a business enterprise is considered a going concern. Accounting periods are artificially defined time frames intended to enable periodic review and reporting. The duty of enterprise management in their capacity as shareholders' agents, is to utilize shareholders funds in a manner that at least long-term opportunity cost of equity is earned. Periodic evaluation structure of EVA® does not align with the long-term going concern principle.

b) Enhancing shareholder value involves decisions and actions in three key strategic areas stated above. Though primarily EVA® intends to measure holistic enterprise performance it fails to actually capture the whole truth, focusing on only two areas – 'operating' and 'financing' - ignoring the third i.e. 'investing' as explained in (c) below.

c) When suitable opportunities are not available for efficient utilization of funds internally, managements must consider equity payouts. Such payouts are the outcome of choosing between keeping shareholders funds invested within the business and allowing it to be invested by the shareholders themselves. For this reason, it should rightly qualify as an investment decision. Compounded returns that shareholders earn on their own from these payouts, continues to create value for them, which wouldn't have been otherwise possible. EVA® does not capture this. If paucity of profitable projects is only temporary, and in that event if managements choose to retain shareholders' funds rather than pay-out, the periodic EVA picture would create a misleading poor impression due to an expanded base capital, disregarding the fact that such retention is only temporary.

d) There could be year-to-year variations in actual operating profits. So long as an adverse annual variation does not threaten the long term goal, it shouldn't be a cause for concern. Measuring year-to-year variations may not convey any meaningful information of the big picture. This is particularly important when strategic planning essentially calls for a long-term perspective. Actual performance too must be evaluated with a long-term and cumulative perspective. The relevant question managements must always ask should be "is the long term value growth at risk?" Annual view of EVA® conflicts with this goal.

e) Creating buffers of high value addition during good times requires vision and talent. Such buffers protect the long term goal. Standalone annual assessments which produce negative EVA® when operating profits are poor, fail to reward such foresights, and unduly reprimand short-term failure.

f) As already explained, WACC per se (which wrongly clubs debt and equity costs together), as well as its equity component obtained from CAPM, does not represent the true and relevant opportunity cost. Any measurement dependent on WACC - such as EVA - would also therefore be misleading.

g) The argument about arithmetic tie between EVA® and NPV (PV of EVA® = NPV) provides no comfort because the tie is an inevitable natural occurrence. It would always occur by default between estimated NPV and estimated PV of EVA®, or between actual NPV and actual PV of EVA® for the project as a whole. It cannot be regarded as a superior design of EVA®. If actual cash flows differ from estimates, variations in EVA® or even negative EVA® would occur in any case.

Value Creation Index (VCI)

A right metric to measure 'value' must fulfill the following key requirements.

a) It should align with strategic investment planning process. This essentially implies that actual performance should be matched against the same benchmark that is applied during capital expenditure planning, in terms of both, delivering minimum long term opportunity cost as well as beating risk. In short it should measure value creation exactly the way it is planned as well as the way it actually happens.

b) It should overcome the limitations in existing methods such as EVA® described above.

c) It should be universally applicable regardless of industry, and easily computable with publicly available data.

d) It should enable inter-company, inter-industry and inter-country comparison.

e) It should supplement stock market indices; provide objective information about value creation to investors, cutting out speculative noise, as well as serve as a managerial performance measurement tool.

Value Creation Index (VCI) fulfills the above goals. It is a simple but comprehensive index that compares delivered returns against expected returns using published financial data. Detailed explanation of the index construction is beyond the scope of this book but has been explained in the author's research monograph titled 'The Timeless Essence of Financial Science'.

 **Think!**

What is the rationale behind measuring value creation on a stand alone periodic basis when the value creation phenomenon is essentially cumulative and long term? Wouldn't lack of an objective, standardized measurement of economic value contribute to 'irrational exuberance' in equity markets and hurt shareholder value when expectations do not materialize?

Epilogue

I hope the questions and issues raised and discussed in this book serves its primary purpose of educating and informing common investors about how public companies manage shareholders' money. The attempt has been to simplify financial concepts that are generally considered as understandable only by experts in the domain. Common investors must understand, question and reason out whether company managements, money managers and investment advisors, whom they trust with their money, truly follow prudent practices towards enhancing shareholder wealth. The fact remains that 'understanding financial markets' has remained shrouded in ambiguity till this day, as has been already pointed out. If financial awareness among investors increases, and the fallacies in corporate finance are understood and eliminated through appropriate regulatory initiatives leading to a financially stable world, I believe the purpose of my effort would be served. I urge interested readers who may wish to delve deeper, to read 'The Timeless Essence of Financial Science'.

About the author

Rajesh D. Mudholkar is a certified Management Accountant with over three decades of professional experience. He brings his knowledge and insights gained from several years of MNC work, teaching finance, quantitative analysis and business research at post-graduate business management programs, and working closely in equity and derivative markets, into his writings. His book 'The Timeless Essence of Financial Science' documents his path-breaking research that resolves decades old flaws in corporate financial practices, the root cause of financial crises. In another book 'The Entrepreneur's Oath' he explains with irrefutable evidences, why caring for people and the planet is the only way business enterprises can achieve sustainable success. He is an alumnus of 'University of Mumbai' and an Associate member of ICAI, India's apex statutory body for Cost and Management Accounting. He lives in India.

He may be reached at: mudholkar.rajesh@gmail.com

www.ingramcontent.com/pod-product-compliance
Lightning Source LLC
Chambersburg PA
CBHW072034190526
45165CB00017B/789